EXTREME SURVIVAL
OCEANS

Sally Morgan

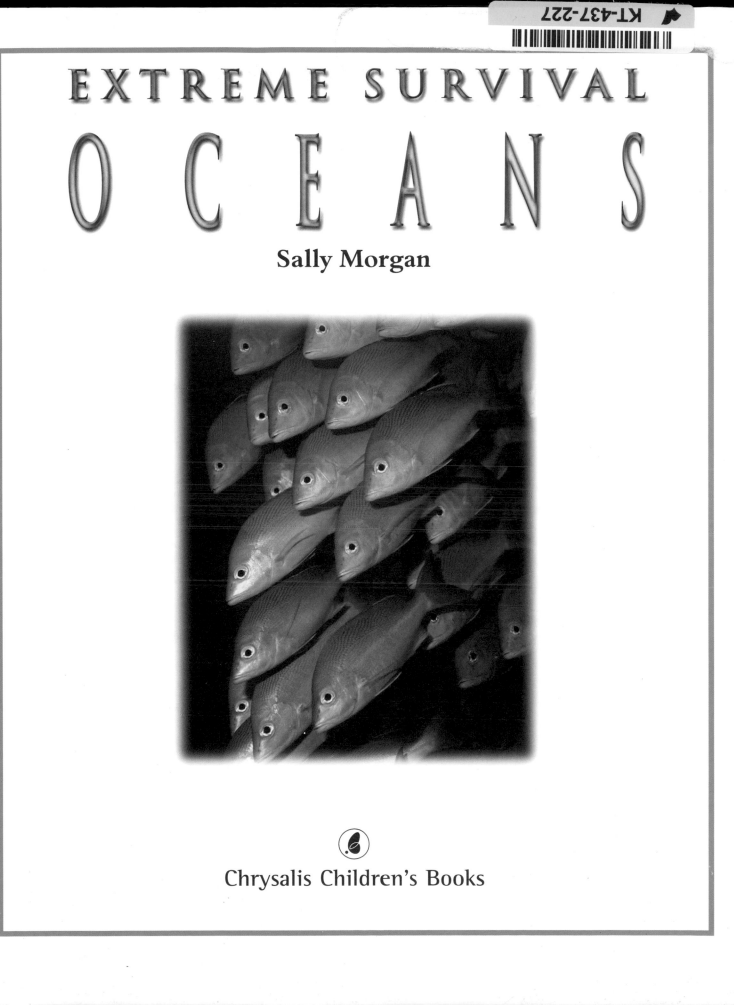

Chrysalis Children's Books

First published in the UK in 2003 by
Chrysalis Children's Books
An imprint of Chrysalis Books Group Plc
The Chrysalis Building, Bramley Road, London W10 6SP

Paperback edition first published in 2005

Design and editorial production
Bender Richardson White, Uxbridge

ISBN 1 84138 700 2 (hb)
ISBN 1 84458 453 4 (pb)

British Library Cataloguing in Publication Data for this book is available from the
British Library.

Printed in China

10 9 8 7 6 5 4 3 2 1

Acknowledgements
We wish to thank the following individuals and organizations for their help and
assistance and for supplying material in their collections:
CORBIS Corporation/Images: pages 1, 9 top (Stephen Frink/CORBIS), 9 bottom
(Stephen Frink/CORBIS), 12 (Amos Nachoum/CORBIS), 13 bottom (Sea World,
Inc/CORBIS), 22 top (Yogi, Inc./CORBIS), 25 left (Chris North; Cordaiy Photo Library
Ltd./CORBIS). Ecoscene: pages 4 (Chinch Gryniewicz), 6 (Papilio/Robert Pickett), 8
(Papilio/Steve Jones), 10 right (Papilio/Robert Pickett), 11, 18 top (John Liddiard), 18
bottom (Justine Pickett), 26 (John Liddiard), 27 (Mark Caney), 28 (Steve Jones), 29
(Jeff Collet), 31 (Steve Jones). Oxford Scientific Films Photo Library: pages 2
(Norbert Wu), 5 (Scott Winer), 14 (Howard Hall), 15 top (Rudie Kuiter), 16 (Clive
Bromhall), 17 top (Norbert Wu), 17 bottom (Paulo de Oliveira), 19 (Doug Allen), 20,
21 top and 21 bottom (Scripps Institute of Oceanography), 23 (Norbert Wu), 24
(David Fleetham), 25 (Michael Pitts/SAL). PhotoDisc Inc.: pages 3 (Mark Downey),
30 (Mark Downey). Still Pictures: pages 7 top (Paul Glendell), 7 bottom (Secret Sea
Vision), 10 left (Paul Glendell), 13 top (Norbert Wu), 22 bottom (Paul Springett),
Cover photos: front: Amos Nachoum/CORBIS, back: Mark Webster. Oxford Scientific
Films Photo Library
Diagrams and maps: Stefan Chabluk.

Editorial Manager: Joyce Bentley
Project Editor: Lionel Bender
Text Editor: Clare Hibbert
Design and Make-up: Ben White
Picture Research: Cathy Stastny
Production: Kim Richardson
Consultant: John Stidworthy

EXTREME FACTS

Look for the ocean wave in boxes like
this. Here you will find extra facts,
stories and information about oceans.

◀ Deep-sea fish have
unusual features that
allow them to survive
in complete darkness
(see page 17).

CONTENTS

▼ An isolated isle and coral reef in the Pacific Ocean (see pages 8–9).

THE OCEANS

The Earth is a watery planet. Oceans cover more than two-thirds of its surface. The water is deep, too. If the ocean floor was level, the depth of water covering its surface would be 3700m.

A huge variety of plants and animals live in the oceans. They range from tiny bacteria to the world's largest animal, the Blue whale. Most are found in the top 200m of the water and around the coasts, where they get plenty of sunlight.

The ocean floor, or bed, is crisscrossed by massive underwater mountain chains, which occasionally poke above the surface as islands. In places, the ocean floor suddenly plunges deep into the Earth, creating immense trenches. The bottom of the deepest of these, the Marianas Trench, is 11 km below the surface of the ocean.

◀ Huge waves, driven by strong winds, batter a shoreline. In a big storm, waves can reach heights of more than 15m.

4

Although the oceans make up so much of Earth, we know surprisingly little about the deepest parts. There is a world of strange-looking animals – some of which we have not even discovered yet.

▶ The force of ocean waves and currents is immense, making survival difficult for marine creatures.

▼ Oceans surround the seven continents, or giant masses of land. Both the Pacific and Atlantic Oceans are often divided into north and south sections. The Arctic Ocean varies in size as much of it freezes over in winter.

DEEPER THAN MOUNTAINS

The largest of the five oceans is the Pacific Ocean. The others, in order of size, are the Atlantic Ocean, the Indian Ocean, the Southern Ocean and the Arctic Ocean.

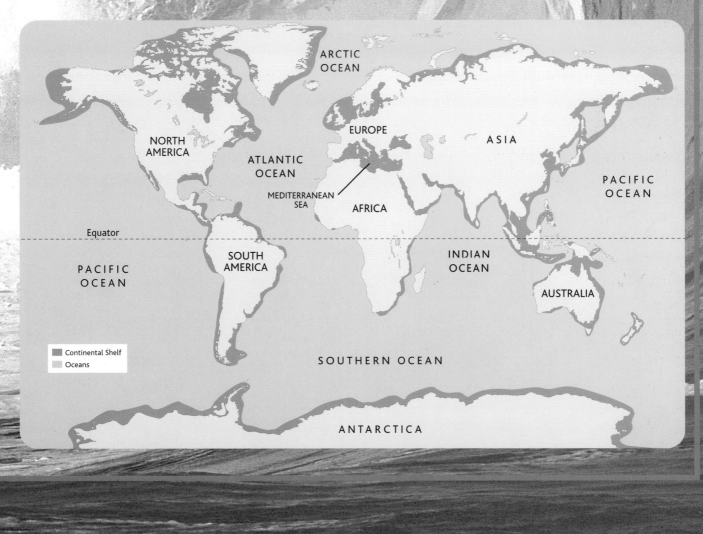

ARCTIC OCEAN

NORTH AMERICA

ATLANTIC OCEAN

EUROPE

ASIA

PACIFIC OCEAN

MEDITERRANEAN SEA

AFRICA

Equator

PACIFIC OCEAN

SOUTH AMERICA

INDIAN OCEAN

AUSTRALIA

SOUTHERN OCEAN

ANTARCTICA

■ Continental Shelf
□ Oceans

LAND MEETS OCEAN

The shallow waters around the continents are full of life – even though the plants and animals are constantly battered by the waves. During low tide, they must survive sun, wind, rain and even snow.

The sea level is constantly changing along the coast. Twice a day, the tide rises up the shore and then goes back again. High tide is when the sea comes up the shore, covering everything with salty water. As the tide starts to go back down the beach, more and more of the shore is left exposed. At low tide, the shore is uncovered. The plants and animals have to survive without water until the next high tide, 12 hours later.

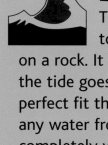

LIMPET SHELLS
The limpet grows its shell to fit in a particular dimple on a rock. It returns to this place when the tide goes out. Its shell is such a perfect fit that the limpet cannot lose any water from its body – it has a completely watertight hiding place!

▶ Barnacles and limpets are found on rocky shores. When the tide goes out, limpets clamp their cone-shaped shell to the rock while barnacles close their lids.

Animals have a variety of ways of surviving low-tide conditions. Mussels and barnacles close their shells to make sure that they do not dry out. When the tide returns, they open their shells and start feeding. Crabs hide in rock pools. These are small pools of water that are trapped by the rocks when the tide goes out. Some seaweeds are covered in a layer of slime that stops them drying out in the Sun.

▼ Crabs, crawfish and lobsters, such as this Spiny lobster, are predators and scavengers, preying on fish and shellfish and picking up scraps of food from the shore.

▶ Kelp is a type of seaweed that grows near the shore. Its long leaves, or fronds, form an underwater forest where animals can hide.

ON A REEF

Coral reefs are the most colourful and varied of all the ocean habitats. There are thousands of different fish darting between colourful corals. Finding shelter in the cracks and crevices are crabs, sponges, sea slugs and other sea creatures.

Coral reefs are found in the tropical parts of the world. They develop and survive only in warm, shallow water where there is plenty of light. The reef builds up from the skeletons of millions of tiny animals called polyps, that are related to sea anemones. New polyps grow on top of the leftover skeletons of polyps that have died.

▼ Coral reefs provide shelter and food for thousands of different types of fish and other sea creatures.

SEA ANEMONE
Sea anemones have tentacles covered in stinging cells. Most animals avoid them, but not the clownfish. It hides among the tentacles! The clownfish's body is covered in slime that protects it from the stings.

▲ The Crown-of-thorns starfish eats coral. When the numbers of this starfish build up, huge areas of coral can be destroyed.

The coral reefs are under threat. In many parts of the world, the polyps have lost their beautiful colours and turned white. This is caused by a tiny rise in the temperature of the water around the reef as a result of changes in the world's climate. Sometimes the polyps recover and regain their colour, but often they die. When this happens, all the reef animals that rely on them die, too. Even when conditions in the ocean are right, it takes thousands of years for new reefs to build up.

▼ The bright colours of this sea slug are a warning to other animals that it is poisonous. It is also a hunter, which uses its razor-sharp teeth to tear into sea anemones.

AT THE SURFACE

Most ocean life is found in the surface waters where there is plenty of light. Here, the water is churned by the waves, which are created by the winds. Below 200m the amount of light fades, until the depths are completely dark.

There are two types of surface life: drifters and swimmers. The drifters are all the plants and animals that float about with the tides and currents, including algae, krill and jellyfish. The swimmers power themselves through the water. They include fish, squid, whales and dolphins. There are more than 13 000 types of fish in the oceans, from huge Whale sharks to tiny gobies that are less than a centimetre long.

▼ Drifters include these tiny shellfish, which have been magnified under a microscope. Tiny ocean animals form part of the plankton.

▲ A Compass jellyfish floats near the surface. It drifts slowly, carried by the currents.

▼ Humpback whales feed on krill. They take in huge mouthfuls of water and sieve out the tiny shrimp-like animals.

Like plants on land, the drifting algae use sunlight to make food. In turn, the algae are eaten by tiny animals, such as the shrimp-like krill. Krill are eaten by larger animals, including fish and whales.

Many fish prefer to feed at the surface at night. During the day they sink to darker parts of the ocean, where hunters find them harder to see.

 MARINE MAMMALS
Dolphins, seals and whales live in water but they have lungs just like humans. They have to come to the surface to breathe. Unlike humans, many of them can survive underwater for up to 30 minutes – some can even last for two hours on one lungful of air!

IN MID-OCEAN

The oceans are home to some of the world's largest animals. They travel great distances in their search for food. They survive by eating a very wide variety of food.

Strangely, many of the largest animals feed on the smallest ones. Whale sharks, Basking sharks, Manta rays and some of the huge whales all feed on tiny, drifting sea creatures, or plankton. They must swim over long distances to find enough food to survive.

▼ The Great white shark is a fearsome predator. It has a wide jaw and rows of sharp teeth. The teeth are like hooks, for extra grip.

RECORD BREAKERS
The Whale shark is the world's largest fish. It is as long as four cars and weighs over 12 tonnes. The fastest fish is the sailfish. It could do 13 laps of a swimming pool in the time it took an Olympic champion to swim one!

Predators are animals that hunt. The animals they hunt are called prey. In the sea, predators are usually powerful swimmers with streamlined bodies that slip through the water. Sailfish, marlin and tuna can chase after prey at speeds of over 100 km/h.

The oceans are huge, however. A fish can swim for many kilometres without coming across any prey at all. It is hard to see in the water. Hunters rely on their sense of smell and also pick up movements in the water. Sharks and rays have an extra sense. They can detect the electric signals created when all animals move their muscles.

◄ Remoras are ocean hitchhikers. These fish hitch a ride on larger ones, such as sharks and rays, using their sucker-like mouths to hang on. Once their carrier finds food, the remoras will let go and feed on the scraps. This remora, with open mouth, is seen from below.

▼ Manta rays use their giant 'wings' to push themselves through the water.

TWILIGHT ZONE

As you move down into deeper water, it gets darker and colder. That is because the light and warmth from the Sun cannot reach down that far.

The deep ocean begins just a few hundred metres below the surface. The top part is called the twilight zone. It is chilly and gloomy, but there are still a few faint glimmers of light. The animals that live here have to survive the cold and lack of light. Many of them have large eyes to make the most of the little light there is. Some animals have see-through bodies, so they are even harder for predators to spot.

▼ Sperm whales often feed in the twilight and dark zones but need to come to the surface to breathe. The deepest dive recorded by a Sperm whale is 2250m – greater than any other animal.

Animals of the twilight zone must cope with another problem – pressure. When you try to swim underwater, sometimes your ears hurt. The weight of all the air and water is pressing down on you. Pressure becomes greater the deeper you go. If it travelled down 1000m, a fish from the surface would be crushed by the pressure. But the animals that live in the deep are adapted to survive the high pressure. If they are brought to the surface, they explode.

◀ The cuttlefish is related to squid and octopus. It uses its huge eyes to locate prey and its ten arm-like tentacles to capture them and bring them to its mouth. Cuttlefish feed on fish and shellfish.

▶ The intertidal zone is that part of the shore between high and low tide levels. The continental shelf is the gently sloping floor of the ocean surrounding the continents. The width of the shelf varies from almost nothing to 1200 km. The continental slope joins the continental shelf to the ocean floor.

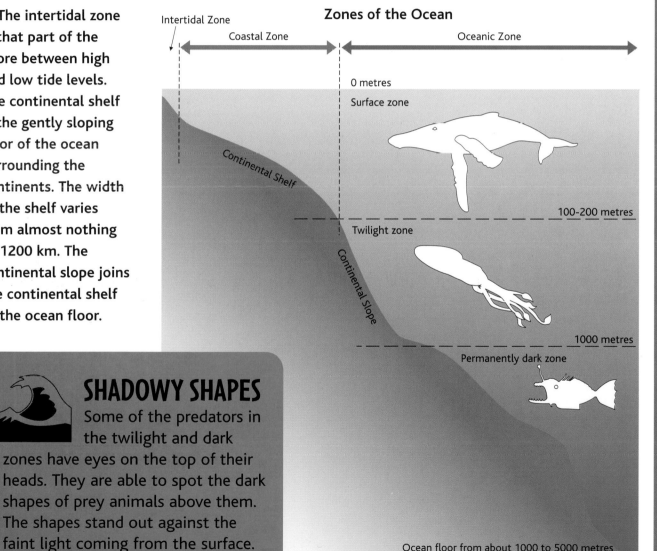

Zones of the Ocean

Intertidal Zone

Coastal Zone

Oceanic Zone

0 metres

Surface zone

Continental Shelf

100-200 metres

Twilight zone

Continental Slope

1000 metres

Permanently dark zone

Ocean floor from about 1000 to 5000 metres

SHADOWY SHAPES

Some of the predators in the twilight and dark zones have eyes on the top of their heads. They are able to spot the dark shapes of prey animals above them. The shapes stand out against the faint light coming from the surface.

15

THE DEEP UNKNOWN

Below about 1000m is the dark zone, where the ocean is pitch-black and cold. It looks like an eerie, empty world, but even in this extreme environment some amazing animals can survive.

The biggest problem facing animals of the deep is the lack of food. Only a few scraps of food sink down from above, and it is hard to find prey. Most deep-sea fish have sharp teeth, big mouths and stretchy stomachs. When a Gulper eel or Deep-sea swallower does manage to catch prey, it swallows it whole.

▼ In the dark zone, because it is hard to find a mate, some types of male anglerfish make sure they do not lose a female they encounter. They attach themselves to her back – permanently. Here two males – each one is very small – are attached to a female.

▼ The Deep-sea swallower is almost all mouth! It unhinges its jaws to fit around prey bigger than itself and then its stomach stretches to fit.

GLOWS IN THE GLOOM

It may be pitch-black in the deep, but some animals can make their own glowing light. Several of them can switch their light-producing organs on and off. Many of these animals use the light to attract prey. Others use it to scare away predators.

▲ Deep-sea fish may have small bodies but their teeth look formidable! Few animals can escape jaws like those of this 'bristlemouth' fish.

The dark zone is so dark there is no need for camouflage. Most of the animals are black or dark red. Some choose not to waste energy by swimming around looking for food. Instead, they stay still in the water and wait for prey to swim past. They cannot see anything, but they can sense movement. One of the best at this is the Hairy anglerfish. Its body is covered in a tangle of whiskery feelers that can detect the tiniest movements.

OCEAN FLOOR

The ocean floor extends between continental shelves. It can be rocky or covered in thick, muddy ooze. Often there is nowhere for animals to hide from predators.

There is a constant rain of material falling to the ocean floor from the open waters above. This is known as marine snow. It includes scraps of dead seaweed, shells, plankton and, sometimes, the bodies of large animals. None of this goes to waste. It provides food for all sorts of bottom-dwelling animals.

▲ Brittle stars are related to starfish. They have long, thin arms that pull their small bodies across the ocean floor. Brittle stars are predators that feed on small animals.

▲ The sea cucumber is a sausage-shaped animal. Around its mouth it has sticky tentacles that suck up food from the ocean floor.

Many animals at the bottom filter food from the water. The tubeworm has sticky tentacles to trap plankton. Sea lilies are animals that have cup-shaped bodies and a mass of feathery arms that sweep food towards their mouths. Some animals, such as amphipods, build tunnels in the sand. They suck in water, filter food particles from it and then pump out the waste.

There are predators on the ocean floor, too, including flatfish, crabs, lobsters, rays and sharks. Some flatfish bury themselves in the sand and wait for prey animals to come along.

MUD MONSTER

The Grey whale dives down to hunt bottom-dwelling amphipods – animals related to prawns that feed in the mud. The whale scoops up huge mouthfuls of sludge. It has sieves in its mouth that trap the wriggling amphipods.

▼ This isopod – a shrimp-like animal – lives in the freezing cold waters of the Antarctic. It is related to the woodlice found on land. It filters food from the mud on the ocean floor.

HOT SPOTS

The deepest parts of the ocean contain some of the most extreme places where animals survive. Dotted along the rocky ocean floor are cracks in the Earth from which gush clouds of boiling-hot water, full of poisonous chemicals.

Around these hot-spots it is pitch-black and the pressure is 250 times greater than at sea level. The water also contains poisons called sulphides. Even though it is at boiling point – or even hotter – just a few centimetres away the water may be icy cold. These conditions seem too impossible for any life to cope with, but some creatures do make their home here.

▶ The giant tubeworms around this vent, or gush of boiling water, are as tall as a room. The red tips take in oxygen from the water.

 BLACK SMOKERS
Along with the scalding water, the hot-spots squirt out specks of dark mud. Over the years these pile up to build dark chimney stacks. The stacks are nicknamed 'black smokers' and some are as tall as tower blocks.

Bacteria – the simplest living things there are – are able to feed off the sulphides. In turn, these bacteria feed other animals living around the hot-spot. There are giant tubeworms that do not have a mouth or gut. Instead, they get their food from the millions of bacteria that live within their body. The bacteria feed many other types of animal, too, including shrimps, crabs, fish, sea anemones, mussels and clams.

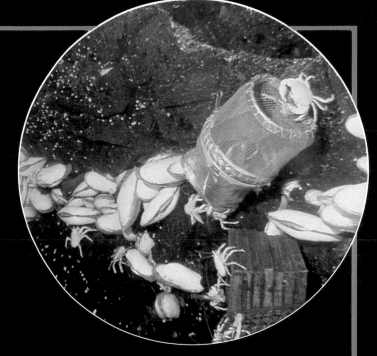

▼ This stalked hydroid is related to jellyfish and anemones. The tentacles around its mouth are covered in tiny sting cells which contain poison. It feeds on small animals in the water.

▲ Scientists gather clams and crabs like these from deep-sea hot spots in order to learn more about them.

DIVING IN

Emperor penguins, seals and whales can dive to great depths, but diving deep is more dangerous for humans. Our bodies are not designed to cope with the lack of air, the cold, the salt and the pressure.

Swimmers and snorkellers can dive under the water but they have to return to the surface to breathe. Scuba divers carry tanks of air so they can breathe underwater. This means they can stay under much longer. They can dive as deep as 60m quite safely, and one scuba diver is on record for diving down to 145m.

▼ Scuba divers must keep track of how long the air in their breathing tanks will last under water.

▶ This diver came up too quickly. This special chamber will help him get used to the pressure change.

PEARL DIVERS

Female pearl divers collect pearls from oysters on the sea bed. They might make 100 dives in a day without air tanks, each time just holding their breath. They take care not to swallow sea water; the human body cannot cope with the salt in seawater.

For deeper dives, a diver wears a helmet diving suit. The suit covers the diver except for the head and hands. It is waterproof, so no water can reach the skin. The helmet is made of metal or plastic. It is attached to the suit. There is a pipe to the helmet that carries air from a breathing tank carried on the diver's back.

Divers have to take care when they come back up to the surface. If they come up too quickly from where the pressure was high, it can make them very sick.

▶ A deep-sea diver wears a dry suit and a pressure-resistant hard helmet. The suit keeps the body dry and warm in cold water.

EXPLORING THE DEEP

Divers can only stay underwater for a short time and they cannot reach the deepest parts of the ocean. Deep-sea exploration is carried out in mini-submarines called submersibles, or 'subs'.

▼ Some subs take tourists underwater to view coral reefs. This one is called *Atlantis* and is based in Hawaii.

Submersibles are fitted with lights, cameras and robot arms that can pick up objects or carry out repair work. Inside, the pressure is kept at normal levels so people do not get sick. The pressure pushes on the walls of the sub and not on the people inside. The walls and portholes are made of strong steel and extremely thick glass so they can withstand the immense pressure. Because of the dangers and expense, the latest submersibles do not carry people. They are controlled by people at the surface.

▲ *Alvin* is a submersible, developed in the 1980s, that can dive to 4500m and carry up to three people. *Alvin* has been used to explore hot spots on the ocean floor and the wreck of the *Titanic*.

◄ Submersibles can go far deeper than deep-sea divers. They are used to check and repair oil rigs and lay pipelines.

NUCLEAR SUBMARINES

The latest nuclear-powered submarines are the largest of all submersibles. They are up to 170m long and can go down to depths of 300m. With full supplies for the crew, they can stay under for months at a time.

There is also an underwater laboratory, called *Aquarius*, in waters off the coast of Florida in the United States. Scientists visit it to study ocean life and to learn how the human body copes with living at high pressure. They spend up to ten days there. It is so much like living in a spaceship that teams of astronauts have gone to train in *Aquarius*.

OCEANS: FACTS

UNDERWATER MOUNTAINS
The deep-sea floor is broken up by a chain of mountains called the Mid-Ocean Ridge. The mountains are about 3000m high, 50 km wide and 60 000 km long. They snake through the Atlantic, Pacific, Indian and Arctic Oceans.

SCARY STINGER
The Box jellyfish is found in shallow waters off Australia. Fully grown, it is as big as a basketball and has up to 60 tentacles, each 5m long and carrying poison. Just brushing against the tentacles would be enough to kill you in four minutes.

COLD SEEPS
As well as hot-spots on the ocean floor, scientists have discovered super-cold spots, where there are poisonous snowballs on the floor. Living in this strange environment are new species of worms, nicknamed ice worms. There are also enormous tubeworms that are hundreds of metres long.

MONSTER OF THE DEEP
The Giant squid is about 15m long and weighs as much as an elephant. Nobody has ever seen one alive. Its eyes are the size of dinner plates, which suggests that it lives in the twilight zone.

◄ An aerial view of part of the Great Barrier Reef off the north-east coast of Australia. It is the world's largest single system of coral reefs, extending more than 1930 km.

THE DEEP UNKNOWN

So far, scientists have explored just 10 sq km of the deep-sea floor. That means there are another 300 million sq km to go!

UNDERWATER LIVING

French ocean expert Jacques Cousteau made TV programmes about the undersea world and also invented the aqualung, an air tank for divers. In 1962 he launched *Conshelf One,* a house 10m under the sea. Two divers, Albert Falco and Claude Wesly, spent a week there. The next year Cousteau spent a month in *Starfish House,* part of an underwater village on the floor of the Red Sea.

REACHING THE DEEP

In 1960 a craft called *Trieste* went down 11 km to the bottom of the Marianas Trench in the Pacific Ocean. The men onboard, Jacques Piccard and Don Walsh, are the only people to have reached the deepest spot in the ocean. As the craft carried them down, they could hear its metal walls cracking under the pressure!

▼ A diver's face mask has a viewing window designed for use under water. Rays of light from the sky are bent as they enter water and ocean currents disturb the rays, but divers can see clearly through their masks.

OCEANS: SUMMARY

Oceans present living things with extreme conditions ranging from lack of sunlight, churning water, great pressure, strong currents and ever-changing temperatures.

Creatures such as plankton, certain fish and tubeworms spend all their lives in one area of ocean and so avoid the constantly changing conditions. Whales and seals are adapted to cope with some extremes and can move freely through the oceans. Coral reefs and the wildlife that lives on them are especially adapted to a very limited range of ocean conditions. Disturbance or pollution of the reefs by people can injure or kill them quickly and they take many thousands of years to recover, if ever. People can survive in oceans only with the aid of special equipment.

▼ Exploring ocean shipwrecks – like this one off the coast of Egypt – and underwater archaeology, studying the remains of harbours and towns that were once above sea level, are exciting and dangerous.

OCEANS: ON THE WEB

If you have access to the Internet, look up these websites or use a search engine and type in keywords such as 'oceans' and 'diving', to find out more.

The Coral Reef Alliance
www.coralreefalliance.org
Site dedicated to protecting coral reefs.

Philippe Cousteau Foundation
www.cousteaufoundation.org
This foundation was set up by the son of Jacques Cousteau to further ocean exploration.

Center for Marine Conservation
www.cmc-ocean.org
Website for a charity that aims to protect ocean wildlife.

Aquarius
www.uncwil.edu/nurc/aquarius
All about *Aquarius*, the underwater laboratory off the coast of Florida. This website has expedition diaries, photos and live views of what is going on in the lab right now.

Woods Hole Oceanography Institute
science.whoi.edu/DiveDiscover
A website that follows expeditions to the ocean floor and provides information on the latest deep-sea research.

Abyss Live
www.bbc.co.uk/nature/programmes/tv/
    abysslive
This website covers a BBC programme which followed three different submersibles down to the ocean floor.

▲ Bright blue starfish are just one of the colourful animals found on this coral reef in Indonesia in the Indian Ocean.

OCEANS: WORDS

This glossary explains some of the words used in this book that you might not have seen before.

Aqualung

a tank filled with squashed air that divers carry so they can breathe underwater.

Black smoker

a chimney-like structure on the ocean floor, formed from a pile up of grains squirted out of the Earth along with hot water.

Camouflage

where an animal's pattern or colouring blends in with its background.

Chemical

any one of the basic elements, such as iron, sodium, oxygen and hydrogen, or mixtures of them.

Coral reef

a mass of 'rock' made up of the skeletons of millions of tiny creatures, called polyps.

Coral reefs take thousands of years to build up and are found only in warm, shallow waters.

Currents

movements of water flowing through the oceans that can carry along marine animals and plants.

▼ Aerial view over a Pacific Ocean island surrounded by a coral reef.

Filter

to take solid bits out of the water. Many sea creatures feed by sieving the water for solid scraps of food.

Isopod

small animal, related to woodlice and pill bugs, which lives near the ocean floor finding food in the mud.

Krill

a small shrimp-like animal that is a popular food for many whales.

Marine

to do with the oceans.

Plankton

tiny plants and animals that float in water near the surface and are carried by the currents.

Predator

an animal that hunts other animals for food.

Pressure

a force that presses down on things. In the oceans, pressure increases the deeper you go.

Prey

an animal that is hunted (by a predator) for food.

Submersible

a small, sturdy submarine, able to travel down to great depths.

Tide

the rise and fall of the sea that happens every 12 hours.

Trench

a deep groove in the ocean bed.

Tropical

describes the warmest parts of the world or animals and plants that come from there.

▼ Soft corals have a flexible outer covering, allowing them to move in the currents.

INDEX